This colourful book introduces young children to the idea of time in relation to things that they do, see and experience throughout a day.

For each hour, the pictures illustrate a variety of activities which could be taking place and the simple text asks a question designed to promote discussion about the child's own experiences.

*Available in Series S808*

* **a is for apple**
* **I can count**
**Tell me the time**
**Colours and shapes**
* **Nursery Rhymes**

*Also available as* Ladybird Teaching Friezes

First Edition

# Tell me the time

written by LYNNE BRADBURY

illustrated by LYNN N GRUNDY

Ladybird Books  Loughborough

# Tell me the time... it's 7 o'clock

Time to wake up.
Get out of bed
and get washed.
Can you get dressed by yourself?

# Tell me the time ... it's 8 o'clock

Time for breakfast.
You could have cornflakes or eggs
or toast or fruit.
What do you like to eat for breakfast?

# Tell me the time ... it's 9 o'clock

Time to wash the dishes.
Dry the spoons; dry the cups.
How many plates?
Do you help to wash and dry the dishes?

# Tell me the time... it's 10 o'cloc

Time to go out and play.
Play with your toys; ride your bike;
run with your friends.
What games do you like to play?

# Tell me the time... it's 11 o'clock

Time for a drink.
You could have milk or orange juice.
Mum and Dad like coffee.
What do you like to drink?

# Tell me the time... it's 12 o'cloc

Time to help Mum and Dad.
Dad is working indoors.
Mum is cleaning the car.
Do you like to help at home?

# Tell me the time... it's 1 o'clock

Time to have something to eat.
Eat it all up, it might be your favourite next
Everyone is hungry.
What do you like to eat?

# Tell me the time... it's 2 o'clock

Time to go to the shops.
Buy some food; buy some new shoes.
The bags are very heavy.
Do you like to go shopping?

# Tell me the time... it's 3 o'clock

Time to play with your friends.
Play on the swings or
go down the slide.
What do you do in the park?

# Tell me the time... it's 4 o'clock

Time for your television programme,
or you could look at a book
or draw a picture.
What do you like to watch on television?

# Tell me the time... it's 5 o'clock

Today is special. It's time for a party.
Lots of food and games
with your friends.
Have you been to a party?

Happy
Birthday

# Tell me the time... it's 6 o'clock

Time to get ready for bed.
Get undressed; have a bath.
It's time for a story.
Which is your favourite story?

# Tell me the time... it's 7 o'clock

Time to go to sleep.
It's been a very busy day.
Goodnight, see you tomorrow!